Also by Eve Arnold

The Unretouched Woman

THIS IS A BORZOI BOOK

PUBLISHED IN NEW YORK BY ALFRED A. KNOPF

FLASHBACK!

Eve Arnold

FLASHBACK! The 50's

ALFRED A. KNOPF · NEW YORK · 1978

This Is a Borzoi Book

Published by Alfred A. Knopf, Inc.

Copyright © 1978 by Eve Arnold

All rights reserved under International and Pan-American Copyright Conventions.

Published in the United States by Alfred A. Knopf, Inc., New York, and

simultaneously in Canada by Random House of Canada Limited, Toronto.

Distributed by Random House, Inc., New York.

Library of Congress Cataloging in Publication Data

Arnold, Eve.

Flashback! The 50's.

1. United States—History—1945–1953—Pictorial works.
2. United States—History—1953–1961—Pictorial works.
3. Arnold, Eve.   I. Title.

E813.A83 1978   779'.9'9739   78-54901

ISBN 0-394-50043-1

Manufactured in the United States of America

FIRST EDITION

For Michael the Younger;
For Michael the Elder; and
For the ganze Meshpocha in between—
By blood, by marriage, and by chance

FLASHBACK!

I returned home to the United States after living abroad for sixteen years. I walked the streets of New York completely beguiled by the changes time had brought. Social attitudes were greatly altered. It would have been unthinkable in the 1950's to see blacks and whites walking hand in hand, homosexuals together openly, men with shoulder-length hair, or women with breasts swinging free, unconfined by brassieres or not exaggerated by "falsies."

"Falsies," I thought. "A 50's word." As I conjured up that decade when I had worked as a photographer in America, other catchwords came. I played a stream-of-consciousness game with contemporaries. "What," I asked, "comes to mind if I say 1950's?" Some thought the question too broad, but most came up with single words or phrases that matched the ones that I dredged from my own interior landscape.

Ike, bobby-sox, blacklist, McCarthy, cold war, iron curtain, Marilyn, Korea, togetherness, loyalty oath (a phrase from Harry Truman's 40's but identified more closely with the 50's), rock 'n' roll, Malcolm X, civil rights, Little Rock, short back and sides, duck's ass.

The words brought sounds, and the sounds brought smells, and the smells brought images, and the images reminded me that perhaps I should look at my photographs of that time. I had been witness to that decade of disillusionment; perhaps I ought to go back and see my own pictures, read my own observations of that time written to go with the pictures, in order to see if I could examine *now* in terms of *then*.

I went back to my own files because I felt there was a personal shorthand that might make it easier for me to try to understand much that, living in Europe, I had missed—Watergate, Vietnam, the destruction in the cities, and all the social change I saw about me. Without a background to lay it against, I would be moving in a personal vacuum. I kept telling myself I wasn't going back—just catching up.

My photographs are, of necessity, subjective—filtered through my background and education, my prejudices, and the limitations imposed by chance and the time in which I lived. In 1950 I was inexperienced and young; I moved with the prevailing political and social winds. I did not attempt to catalogue all events and trends, but did try to find a sense of the significance of the time and the people. The choice was purely personal. I chose to photograph Malcolm X rather than Martin Luther King, Jr., the non-violence movement rather than Little Rock.

I ranged from the Malcolm X and the Black Muslim story that stretched over a period of two years to a difficult political story on a McCarthy hearing that took two days. Each story seemed to have its own rhythm and I would have to adjust accordingly. Malcolm would dictate time and place, but McCarthy hearings were a matter of record, and time on these was limited to how long the Wisconsin senator thought he could hold the limelight.

The nature of freelance photography forces the practitioner either to be frenzied with work—and occasional excitement—or to sit around in a panic of boredom wondering whether she has lost her touch. Suddenly the last job is over and the next one hasn't been offered. It doesn't exactly make for a stable life.

Because I always tried to cut down on tension between jobs (and because I preferred working on my own ideas), I always tried to have an independent project on hand. One such went on for ten years. It was in the township of Brookhaven (where my home was)—a twenty-mile-square Long Island area on the Sound. It was about a family called Davis, who were descendants of early American settlers. When we moved there in the early 50's, Brookhaven was pure Americana. The speculators and the developers had not yet arrived to carve it into quarter-acre plots. I knew that it wouldn't last in its American gothic form, and I wanted to record it so that my son, then a baby, would know where he grew up.

I remember the 50's as a corseted time (surely there is a correlation between how people dress and how they think?). The clothes for women first—the cinched-in waist that pushed the breasts up and gave the cleavage, the full-gathered skirts with the full petticoats to make the dress stand out. For sport, there were clam-digger pants, cut loose but narrowing below the calf and exposing part of the shin and the ankle; there were bobby-sox; and, for both sexes, two-toned oxford brogues with white the predominant color. And, for a while, there was a fad of Day-Glo color—brilliant, vibrant, and vulgar, and it glowed in the dark. The men wore pegged trousers.

I found portraiture perhaps the most difficult part of photography. In order to get at the person beneath the surface (and to avoid the standard "mug shot"), I experimented with a portrait-in-action: the subject is absorbed in some activity or is shown against a background that interests him.

I tried to do this when I photographed personalities identified with the 50's—Marilyn Monroe, Mamie Eisenhower, Senator Joe McCarthy, as well as a roster of people who would span a longer period, but who were coming to prominence at the end of the decade—Jackie Kennedy, Andy Warhol, and the young Paul Newman. Then there were the timeless ones, but still of that time, ranging from Cagney and Gable through Auden and Isherwood to Taft and Eisenhower.

Although there were those who made the headlines, names were a small part of the whole. Sure it was interesting to see people sparkling at a black debut at the Waldorf-Astoria or dressed up at art openings in Texas or New York, but for pure spectacle I preferred Black Muslim meetings in Washington, New York, and Chicago, with their white-robed women, Elijah Muhammad with his beaded skull cap, and Malcolm X with his guest George Lincoln Rockwell, the head of the American Nazi Party.

I tried to get a sense of America in that time. I haunted Times Square, did stories on Miss America in Atlantic City, faith healers in Oklahoma, a union dispute about a barmaid in New York. I was always on the hop. My mind jumps from situation to situation just as my work tossed me from place to place. The memories will not come out neatly, either chronologically or geographically. I can only follow my mind's illogic, which throws up moods felt, images experienced, and—I hope—a sense of the time's true atmosphere.

The 1952 Republican Presidential Convention in Chicago was my first political assignment. It was for *Picture Post*, a great British picture journal now, alas, defunct and its presses taken over to print comic books. We have seen so much coverage on the political conventions that they now have become clichés, but in 1952 they were new to TV and to us.

It was at the convention that I saw Senator McCarthy for the first time. It was in the early television days. His face was covered in complete television makeup, and he was wearing a blue shirt—white shirts apparently flare in the brilliant lights. He held in his hand a list to which he referred from time to time. I don't know the words he spoke—and I refuse to look them up—but I hear in my mind's ear: "I hold in my hand a list of 205 pinkos, Commies with which our State Department is riddled." He later changed it to fifty-seven. For five years he would use his fictitious list to terrorize citizens with his brutal tactics. He only seemed sure of himself when he clutched his list. As soon as he put it down, he started to sweat.

I quote from the copy I filed to *Picture Post*: "The Republican Party has called for greater spending for National Security, balancing the budget, and a cut in taxes at the same time. A neat trick if you can do it. It has demanded an immediate end to the war in Korea and threatened all-out war in China. It has declared itself the Peace Party. It has demanded action to contain Russia; free its satellites in a manner which would most certainly result in war. It has demanded close collaboration with European nations in military and economic matters, while writing off Europe as 'spiritually and economically unreliable and bankrupt.'"

Below that, I wrote: "This sort of doubletalk is simply a formality which repeats itself every four years in both major political parties and which nobody takes seriously."

I shot only one picture of Richard Nixon, then a senator, at the convention because I underestimated him and find in some pencil notes written on the plane coming home: "Had an off-the-record drink with Senator Wayne Morse. He is sick about choice of Nixon. Says Republicans have lost election in November because of choice of Nixon; he was offered as a sop to Taft forces."

As soon as General Dwight D. Eisenhower was presented to the convention as the winner, he did an unprecedented thing. In an effort to heal party wounds and to present a united party front, he went immediately to Senator Robert Taft's headquarters so they could make a joint public appearance. Because I had come late—on the day before the end of the convention—the only picture I had of the candidate, who had gone into retirement after the first day, was the standard shot of the winner on the podium with his arms raised, the one photographers call "the armpit." The press were not told that Ike would go to see Taft, but I played a hunch that he might.

At Taft's headquarters at the Blackstone Hotel, his supporters were angry and defeated. Men were saying it was the end of the Republican Party. Women were in tears. CBS was setting up its TV lights. Ike came in, beaming like the canary that ate the cat. Taft managed a small smile, and the press closed in. Lucky for me that the CBS men, who had set up the lights and formed a cordon (with the police) so their men could work, took pity on my size (5 feet 2½ inches), winked at me, and let me inside their circle for my picture.

Ike kept beaming and delivering well-chosen platitudes. (During the election campaign, one reporter was to groan, as Ike spoke on Korea, "There he goes—he's crossed the 38th platitude again.")

1952 Republican Presidential Convention

Mamie Eisenhower

Dwight D. Eisenhower

Facing page: Robert Taft

Richard Nixon

Joseph McCarthy

Wayne Morse, right

Looking at the photographs of Ike and Taft, I am reminded that, historically, the Republican Convention really launched live news television in the United States. All over the country people became aware that here was an on-the-spot minute-by-minute approach to news and that its mere transience heightened the drama. After 1952 news presentation was never the same again.

Just as the people were riveted to TV during the 1952 conventions, they also became deeply involved in the new medium during the election. Because there were still relatively few television home sets, people were watching outside radio shops, in bars, restaurants, and hotels. In New York a favorite spot was outside NBC studios, in the lobby of the RCA Building (I have to give them equal billing with CBS), where Dave Garroway gave the morning news and the time.

I did a story on the way TV handled the election. I was excited by my first series of big political assignments. At home we talked endlessly about the strategies of both parties and about the candidates. One day during the campaign when the World Series baseball games were being played, I was hanging over the radio listening to the news when my four-year-old son asked, "Who's winning—the Democrats or the Dodgers?" It was hard to tell the election from the baseball game and the commercial announcements from the news.

Adlai Stevenson

By the time the election was over, I found myself wanting to know more about my own country. I thought that by photographing people in cities with their families and contrasting them with the people I was photographing in the country, where I lived, that I might be well served in learning how to photograph both that which was familiar to me—my home town—and that which was unfamiliar.

There was also a commercial consideration in being able to photograph families. Among the highest-paid assignments were those from the women's magazines—particularly the *Ladies' Home Journal,* which published a series called "How America Lives." The slogan of the magazine was "togetherness." Although I knew the series was a kind of spurious sociology and was really designed to hang features on—the family's food: recipes; the home: furnishings; the family's clothes: fashion; the family's budget: finance—I was anxious to be asked to do a feature for them.

I told this to an editor friend on one of the small magazines—*Coronet.* So I could have a portfolio of similar work to show, he offered me a story on a blue-collar family in Hoboken, New Jersey. I parlayed this into another assignment for *Coronet* on a sailor's family in Newport News,

Virginia. On the basis of these stories, *Fortune* magazine asked me to photograph a junior executive for a giant corporation (his branch of the company sold fertilizers). He lived in a huge complex of apartments—Stuyvesant Town in New York City. When I looked at the pictures of the junior executive with his family, I felt that they personified the myth the press was trying to build of "happy America." These three white families—petit-bourgeois New York, U.S. Navy Newport News, working-class Hoboken—all shared the same consumers' ideals of plenty that both political parties had promised. When I talked with these families, it was, inevitably, about new cars, new TV sets, and goods—clothes, equipment, etc. We also talked about their children and how they would try to give them advantages they had not had, particularly better educations, to provide their children with opportunities and better lives than they themselves lived.

The terms were vague and undefined, but to me the message was clear that these Americans wanted life to be "good" and life to be "simple" and that this thinking symbolized the mood of the country which had elected Eisenhower and helped create the climate for McCarthyism.

Although I was happy working on my assignments and filling in with my personal projects, I kept watching for a chance to handle a news event. I was particularly anxious to photograph a McCarthy hearing in the Capitol in which he was investigating the question of "subversive" books that his aides Roy M. Cohn and G. David Schine had found on a tour of United States Information Service libraries abroad. The hearings were held in the marble halls that later housed the Watergate hearings.

Cohn and Schine had been lambasted by the European and British press during their whirlwind trip, and it didn't seem a good idea for me to present credentials naming foreign magazines and newspapers that had assigned me. Instead, when I arrived at the Senate Press Office, I decided to tell half the truth. I said I was a freelance who worked for *Fortune, Life,* etc., and that I was interested in the senator. Mr. McCarthy usually screened the people permitted to document his hearings, and the session had already started. My train had been late.

It was interesting to me that McCarthy held up the hearing to come out in the hall to vet me— one lone freelance. He looked me over, asked some cursory questions, said okay but did I know the rules that governed photography at the hearings? Yes, I did know the rules: the witness must be asked for permission. Not once in the two days I was there did anybody (including me) ask for permission before photographing a witness.

McCarthy sat at a huge conference table, flanked by his henchmen Cohn and Schine. Various senators were also seated at the table. Behind McCarthy's head was a carved mahogany slab with two carved eagles as finials and which I can only describe as a giant Abraham Lincoln bed headboard. Behind Cohn's head, there was an unfurled, limp American flag. Facing McCarthy sat the witness. Between McCarthy and the witness, sitting tailor fashion on the floor, power packs on shoulders and Speed Graphics at the ready, were an Associated Press photographer and a United Press photographer. The room was floodlit by the TV lights, and the cameramen were set up. There were assorted secretaries, reporters, police with guns in holsters, and a large audience.

All during the hearing the reporters were tense and restless and kept making bad jokes and circulating all kinds of rumors. One of them was that Lillian Hellman would appear. When the day passed and she hadn't arrived, another rumor started that Dorothy Parker was coming. When she didn't show either, the story went around that her lawyer had sent a cable saying she had amnesia.

At noon we recessed for lunch, but McCarthy stayed behind for his press conference. As I worked, he came over to me (I was the only woman reporter there and he was playing to me). He put his hand on my shoulder and asked me whether I was getting everything I needed. As I started to put my hand up to push his hand away, my brain telegraphed that this wasn't a good idea, and I wound up with my hand over his. I stood paralyzed for a beat, then smiled, thanked him, excused myself, and said I had better get back to work.

When the press conference was over, I went down to the press table in the Senate dining room to have a bowl of the famous bean soup. Of the thirty reporters there, not a single one would speak to me. They had seen me with McCarthy and had thought I was holding hands with him. I was miserable, because these were colleagues and some of them friends I had worked with before, but such was the climate of distrust that I couldn't tell them the truth for fear of betrayal. I began to understand how this man terrorized people into silence.

There are several footnotes to my McCarthy story. One is that when it appeared in Germany, the captions on the pictures were changed to make a pro-McCarthy story of it. And in Italy, for some reason I cannot understand, the magazine that published it created its own closing picture—they posed an Italian girl in a situation that never existed in the United States. She was shown with a sack of mail, with the caption: "These are some of the millions of letters which have come to the White House in a campaign that is called, 'Joe must go.'" Would that it had happened!

Senator McCarthy at Senate hearing press conferen‹

by Cohn, Joe McCarthy, and G. David Schine

Cohn and McCarthy

When I returned to Long Island from Washington, I was so upset I retreated from politics and went back to photographing my township and the Davis family. Their ancestors had been given the deed to their land in 1706 by Queen Anne. Davises now laced the township together: the schoolteacher, who taught in the same schoolhouse for fifty years; the postmaster; the undertaker; the lady who sold the penny candy; the justice of the peace; the librarian; the farmers who employed black migratory labor, who came with the potato harvest and, like the birds, went back South for the winter.

There was always a certain amount of snobbery among the different branches of the Family (I think of it with a capital F). The Miller Place Davises, who tended to be intellectuals and sent their boys to Harvard College, looked down on the Mount Sinai Davises because they were farmers. The Mount Sinai Davises looked down on the Port Jefferson Davises because they were merchants. The Port Jefferson Davises looked down on the Coram Davises because they were politicians. The entire clan usually met only at weddings, clambakes, and funerals.

Over the years I photographed these Davis weddings, clambakes, and funerals; went to the polls on Election Day; chased fires with the volunteers; attended DAR meetings and trials by jury. In my town, this meant trial by a six-man petty jury, with a justice of the peace presiding as judge. Although it was illegal to photograph in a

Election day

Preceding pages: Brookhaven

courthouse, my friends and neighbors were unseeing when I brought my cameras. One trial I photographed was a charge of disorderly conduct brought by the People of the State of New York against one Gerard Joseph Malloy for starting a brawl at Nancy's Tavern, causing a disturbance of the peace in which the words "spick" and "nigger" were used.

When I had had my fill of the courthouse—trial by jury, marriage by the justices of the peace, recording of deeds, and the rest of the paraphernalia that community business entailed—one of the justices, who handled traffic offenses and whom I had not photographed, asked me to be sure to show up on a particular Tuesday night. When I said, alas, I had to be in California on that night, he was hurt and angry. He had had the traffic cops handing out traffic tickets all over the township to make sure he had a good crowd for picture taking on Tuesday night.

I remember other situations from my American chronicle—the church supper to celebrate the 150th anniversary of the church, which looked like any other church supper except that the Davises were sitting next to the graveyard eating their chicken and corn on the cob against a background of the tombstones of their ancestors.

The Davis family seemed to embody all the civic virtues of rectitude, to comprise people deeply involved with their community: schoolteacher, justice of the peace, postmistress; deacons of the Unitarian Church, members of the DAR. They were solid, rooted in that Long Island soil for 250 years, and conscious of their responsibilities.

The Davises guarded their unique position and did not mix with the newcomers. When the summer people started to invade the place and later, when the quarter-acre plot bungalows were set up, they stayed completely aloof.

They looked as if they had been especially bred to live in that community. From the moment I first walked about the town of Brookhaven, I itched to photograph them, but beyond a nod of greeting to pass the time of day, there was no approach. I had to wait for them to accept me. Finally, after I had lived there five years, I was invited to tea by one of the elders of the clan and slowly, slowly they accepted me and the camera.

When I showed *Life* magazine editors an accumulation of years of work on the Family, they could not believe that this was indeed one family living in one township. Before they would consider publication, they sent two researchers out to Brookhaven to check up on me. After they had laid the pictures out for a large photo essay, other researchers went back to check on the original researchers and to check my captions.

One of the Davis ladies I photographed refused to have her picture in the *Life* story. It was a key picture and I was upset, but I knew that I must not urge her and just asked her to think it over. She phoned the next morning and gave grudging consent. She said her grandniece had urged her to consent on the basis that it was all too trivial to care about and that, anyway, nobody would remember her picture. Last week, the niece had continued, *Life* had featured a belly dancer and already people had forgotten her, so why should anyone remember Auntie?

Last day of school

The Prom

Library

Church

Pageant

Not far from my home there was a migratory labor camp, simply called locally the "labor camp" but which my son called "the awful place."

The reason the labor camp had barbed-wire fencing, the white overseer explained to me, was to keep out the black dudes in their fancy cars who came in on Saturday night—payday—to roll the migrants. The dudes also handled the dope, the liquor, and the prostitution, he said. For a month I went there daily to photograph.

I would have thought that with the social changes that have taken place in the United States since the 50's this kind of "awful place" would have gone. But no. In the summer of 1977, twenty-five years later, I saw one just as bad on the route to Amagansett, Long Island.

Long Island migrant labor camp

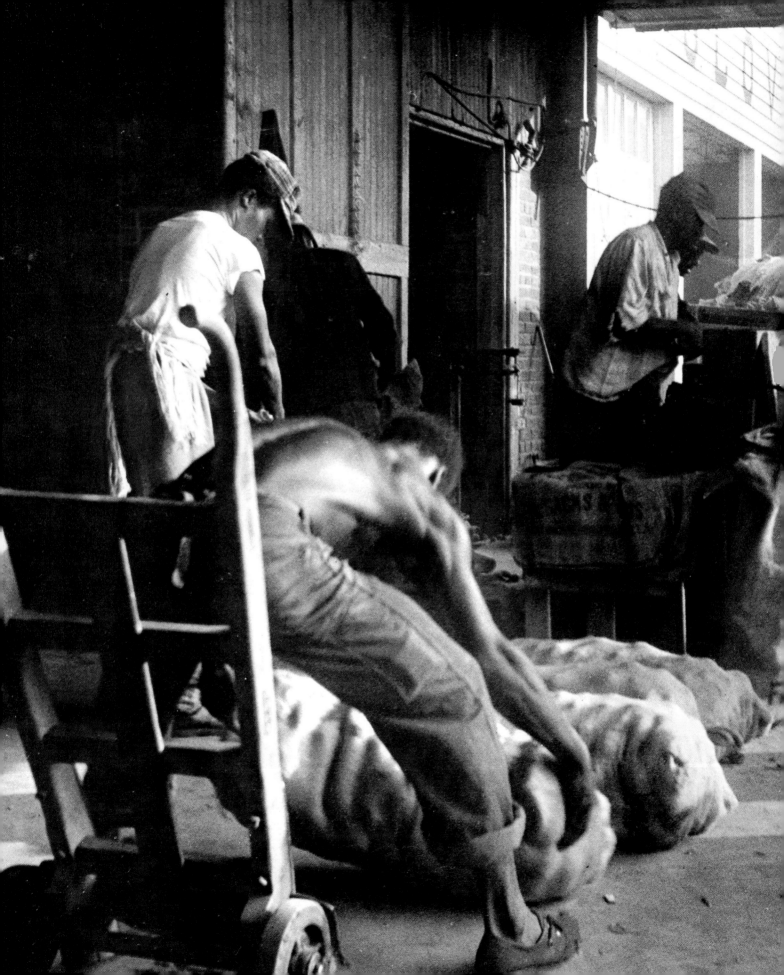

During that time in the 50's cosmetics for blacks were just beginning to be sold in quantity. I had seen these in the shacks of the migrants. They were mainly the brainchild of Rose Morgan (once briefly Mrs. Joe Louis) whose trade name was "Rose Meta." She was also the hair-straightening queen of Harlem. These were the pre-Afro days and a straightening job would cost a housemaid a day's pay every other week.

I went up to Harlem to meet Mrs. Morgan and she invited me to photograph a black debutantes' ball at the Waldorf-Astoria Hotel. In the beginning these black society affairs, like all society affairs, existed to display status, but as the struggle for equality deepened, the balls came to be for raising money for the cause.

Black debutante ball at the Waldorf-Astoria

Mrs. Luci Halm Cullinan, Houston Museum of Fine Arts, Cullinan Gallery

I have always loved watching people in museums, particularly at openings and particularly when they know there is a camera about. There is a studied-unstudied self-consciousness–unself-consciousness going that makes for visual fun. During the decade of the 50's I covered a few openings in both New York and Texas and watched the rich at play.

For me these sessions acted like the sherbet after a heavy course, giving me the stomach to go on with the next heavy course.

René d'Harnoncourt

Mr. and Mrs.
Edward
Steichen

Mary
Rockefeller

And of course, as an antidote to depression, there was always Times Square and Broadway. For a beginning photographer, New York was a total education, not only for its own special tempo and look, but because of the people who roamed the streets, the all-night honky-tonk joints, the flea circus, the dance halls, and the peek-a-boo vending machines. I saw a lot and I learned a lot. I learned how to move quickly, to react instantly, or to wait for the right moment.

I used Times Square as a training ground and I kept going back and back, always exhilarated and stimulated for more.

Flea circus

Peep show

The way for me to learn my craft was by doing—but doing what? In picture journalism that meant events, people, situations, and it meant access. But how? I was naïve enough to move directly toward what I wanted to do.

In the beginning this was difficult because I was not assigned and had no accreditation. I started by calling the publicist of the Metropolitan Opera and showing her the only published story I had—an eight-page layout on fashion shows in Harlem that appeared in *Picture Post*, the British equivalent of *Life*. She was generous and gave me a press pass. Lucky for me—when *Picture Post* saw the pictures, they ran a spread on them.

This gave me the courage to appeal to other publicists and it worked. It gave me freedom to shoot—if I failed, I had no one to answer to but myself, and if I succeeded, I had either material for my portfolio or possibly a published story.

I learned to feel easy when photographing personalities. I was not impressed with the "names" but interested in why they were the chosen ones. Why, for instance, Marilyn Monroe? She was as much part of my need to know as were the migrants and McCarthy. And I felt that with each personality, I did add a cubit to my understanding of the time.

There were endless film openings and promotions in New York, and I seemed to be on every publicist's guest list. I learned a great deal by covering these affairs. The first one I did was a charity benefit in December 1953 for the opening of the film *East of Eden*. Harry Truman's daughter, Margaret, was a sponsor. She wore a ribbon reading USHERETTE across her upholstered chest.

Most of the affairs I was invited to I photographed on speculation, but by the time the assignments came, I had learned enough to turn in work of professional standard. My first assignment was for *Epoca*, an Italian magazine. Silvana Mangano came to New York with her husband, Dino de Laurentiis, the producer, for the opening of his film *War and Peace*. She wanted to hear American jazz. I took her to Columbia Records, where Johnny Mathis sang to her and Dave Brubeck played the piano. They were both astonished at her knowledge of jazz. She matched them song for song and phrase for phrase.

Marilyn Monroe and Arthur Miller

Fleur Cowles, left; Margaret Truman, right

Silvana Mangano, Johnny Mathis, and Dave Brubeck

Jayne Mansfield and Mr. Universe

There was another bonus at the film premiere—Jayne Mansfield squired by Mr. Universe, both of them looking muscle-bound.

As an *aide-mémoire* to the period, my photographic contact books are invaluable. I look at pictures of David Oistrakh, the Russian violinist, and I remember a sudden thaw in American-Soviet relations after Vice President Nixon's visit to Moscow in 1959 and an exchange of artists. I remember that I had been told that I could have fifteen minutes in which to photograph the violinist. He rehearsed for the entire day in a studio in Carnegie Hall and invited me to stay. It was bliss to move about in my stocking feet, trying to be quiet in that tiny rehearsal room while he played and replayed passage after passage of the Beethoven Concerto in D Major. We spoke Yiddish, which he pretended was German. I never asked why, because I knew about Russian anti-Semitism.

I was asked by a British magazine to photograph Christopher Isherwood and W. H. Auden, both resident in the United States. I was in a panic of nerves because I had never photographed important writers before. With a friend, I discussed the problem of how to catch the two in order to show a relationship between them and come away with an interesting shot. My friend suggested that I set them up one behind the other—Isherwood in front and Auden behind, with his hands on Isherwood's shoulders.

When I stammered my way through introductions, I suggested this. My subjects looked at each other, then at me, with distaste. "What does she want?" Isherwood asked. "She wants us to play trains," Auden answered. I suddenly understood. The picture I took was of the pair of them sitting on their roof looking rather grim—Auden's big toe had escaped from its slipper.

The singer Josephine Baker returned to New York to be feted in Harlem after a self-imposed exile of a quarter of a century in Paris. It was both sad and moving because she had either lost touch with the black movement or was not aware of the racial tensions. She rode around Harlem in a white open convertible (it had large placards pasted on its sides with the name of the garage that had lent the car). She did a latter-day "Uncle Tom" act of opening a new furniture department in a white-owned store, and she held a press conference at which the press were served Manischewitz champagne.

David Oistrakh

Christopher Isherwood and W. H. Auden

Josephine Baker

There was another press conference that stays in the mind—one Marilyn Monroe held at the Waldorf-Astoria Hotel to launch a new business venture in which she was president of her own producing company and Milton Greene, its vice president. Their first film was *Bus Stop* and their second one, which they were promoting, was Terence Rattigan's *The Prince and the Showgirl,* to be made in England with Sir Laurence Olivier. In typical M.M. fashion, she kept Olivier and Rattigan cooling outside her door while she dithered inside, unable to decide what to wear. The press waited patiently—finally she posed dramatically on a balcony with Olivier, Rattigan, and Greene; then with only Olivier; then came down a marble staircase gowned (at eleven in the morning) in a long, black velvet frock showing a large expanse of neck, shoulders, and bosom, the dress held up by the equivalent of two very thin shoelaces. She sat down, and Olivier started answering questions the press put to him. She suddenly got bored by it all, leaned forward as though on cue (she later told me she had planned it), and broke one of the slender straps. Safety pins were produced, laughter was heard, the press stopped the serious questions to Olivier, and she proceeded with the business at hand—charming the press, one hand holding the strap, and a frustrated Olivier holding the microphone for her.

Laurence Olivier and Marilyn Monroe

The thought of Marilyn Monroe as a business executive conjures up another business lady—Joan Crawford, as a member of the board of the Pepsi-Cola Company, surrounded by other members of the board at the usual outsize table, this one covered with papers and with open Pepsi bottles placed at intervals. The president of Pepsi is glugging down the stuff. It is 1959. Joan is dressed in black, with a small black hat decorated by a cloth rose, playing the Widow Steele to the armpits. She is recently bereaved. Al Steele, her late husband, had been the chief executive at Pepsi-Cola.

I remember something else. The first time I met Joan, she stormed into Tina Leser's (the dress designer), where I was to photograph her. She was so angry that her hands shook and the tiny poodles that she wore like twin muffs yapped, cowered, and danced around on her wrists. She had come from the Actors Studio, where she had

seen Marilyn Monroe. Joan kept sputtering over and over again: "She doesn't even wear a girdle. Her ass was hanging out. She's a disgrace to the industry!"

It was the first time I had ever heard the term "the industry"—as though there was only one industry in the world—used to mean the film industry. I learned about the industry through both of these ladies. I was to spend a month in 1959 in Hollywood photographing Joan for *Life*. She was making a film called *The Best of Everything*. I spent another two months in 1960 divided between Nevada and Hollywood, photographing Marilyn working on *The Misfits*. But that was at the end of the decade.

I recall the opening night on Broadway in 1953 of Arthur Miller's play *The Crucible*—a courageous attempt to show McCarthyism through parallels with the Salem witch trials in 1692. When we left the theater that night, elated that the play had gone well (I had been documenting it for *Look* magazine), there was a small group of people at the stage door. "Well-wishers," I thought. Not so. They yelled abuse at Arthur Miller and called him a Communist.

I went to Martha's Vineyard to photograph James Cagney. He, his wife, and children did a bit of hoofing in the barn. His wife had been a dancer, but he was teaching his son and daughter. He clowned a lot. For all his lightness of spirit, Cagney was deadly serious about conservation— the word we used before the media got hold of

"ecology." He ran a small farm and loved every rock and weed on it. He made a study of soil conservation. I remember how eloquent he was when he spoke to me about erosion and people's callous unawareness of what they were doing to the environment. I listened, but it didn't really register until years later.

There were many assignments to photograph actors and performers: Mary Martin singing to the children; the Lunts in their Genesee Depot home in Wisconsin; Margaret Sullavan in rehearsal in her new play in New Haven two days before her death; Gwen Verdon rehearsing her dance numbers; the young, then-unknown Paul Newman at the Actors Studio looking tough and showing authority; and of course there was Clark Gable in his dressing room.

There were other personalities in the news— or about to be, as in Andy Warhol's case—Rocky Marciano, the world heavyweight boxing champion; William Carlos Williams, the poet; Alistair Cooke, the journalist and broadcaster posing for *Esquire* as a "best-dressed man" before his "Omnibus" program; and I. I. Rabi, Nobel laureate in physics and one of President Eisenhower's top science advisers. While I was photographing Rabi, he spoke about Russia's space technology and the recently launched Sputnik I: "The reason Russia is ahead of us is that this is the area in which they placed greatest emphasis. We placed a greater premium on material comfort. We have the best, the most modern cars. It is a matter of emphasis."

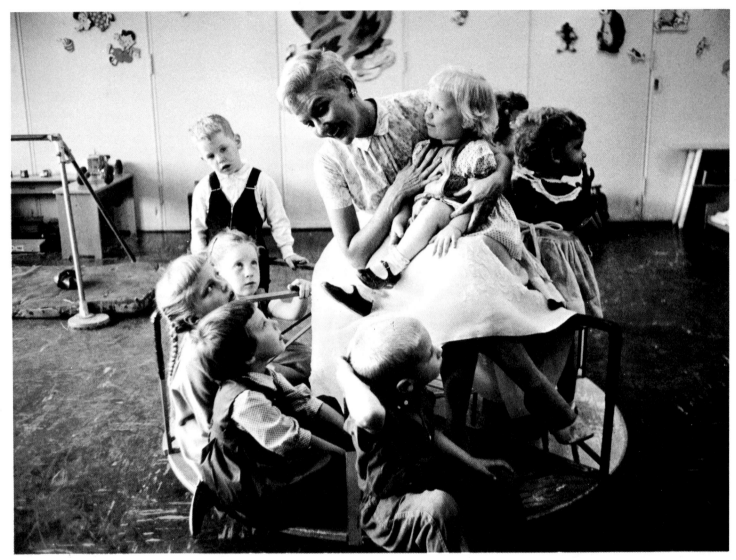

Mary Martin

Lynn Fontanne and Alfred Lunt

William Carlos Williams

Andy Warhol

Margaret Sullavan

Paul Newman at the Actors Studio

Clark Gable

Alistair Cooke

Rocky Marciano

Gwen Verdon

I. I. Rabi

Oral Roberts

During these years I seemed to be dashing around the country from story to story; assignments came not only from magazines, but from public relations firms anxious to publicize their clients. One such unlikely assignment, later to appear in *Fortune* under the title "Saving Souls Is Big Business," was a picture story on Oral Roberts, the faith healer. For this, I went with the writer Jeannie Sakol to Tulsa, Oklahoma, where Roberts had his huge, block-square, windowless, air-conditioned office, and to Cincinnati to a tent meeting of thirty thousand people. We also photographed him on his Oklahoma farm at the entrance to which there was a sign that said, OUR CATTLE BELONG TO THE LORD. When I met him first in Tulsa, he was doing a recorded radio broadcast. Most of his preaching was done for radio or television, and he would urge his listeners to put their hands on the radio or TV set and then he would exhort the Lord: "Lord, Lord, heal, heal this sinner." Because in most states it was illegal for him to solicit money, he would ask people to send him their "letters of support," and the money came pouring in.

Roberts' following was second only to that of Billy Graham. At the tent meetings, people came from all over the United States bringing the sick and the dying for the laying on of his hands. He demonstrated cures, using as ex-

amples people who came up to his pulpit (all of it being filmed for his paid transmission later) to bear witness. The expected cures of deafness, alcoholism, and other possibly psychosomatic illnesses were routine, but occasionally there was the dramatic crippled figure who got up from a wheelchair and walked to the accompaniment of cries of "Hallelujah!" and of tears. While all the hoopla was going on in the main tent, the real sufferers, who had been brought on stretchers by plane, train, and ambulance, waited in a smaller tent for Oral Roberts to come through and touch them. The laying on of his hands was quite an experience. I know, because when I met him, he demonstrated it on my back, and I felt so elated that Jeannie and I speculated that he must have trained as an osteopath.

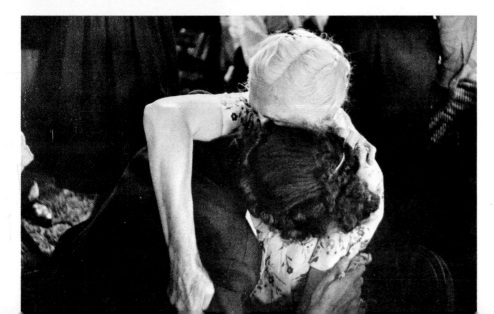

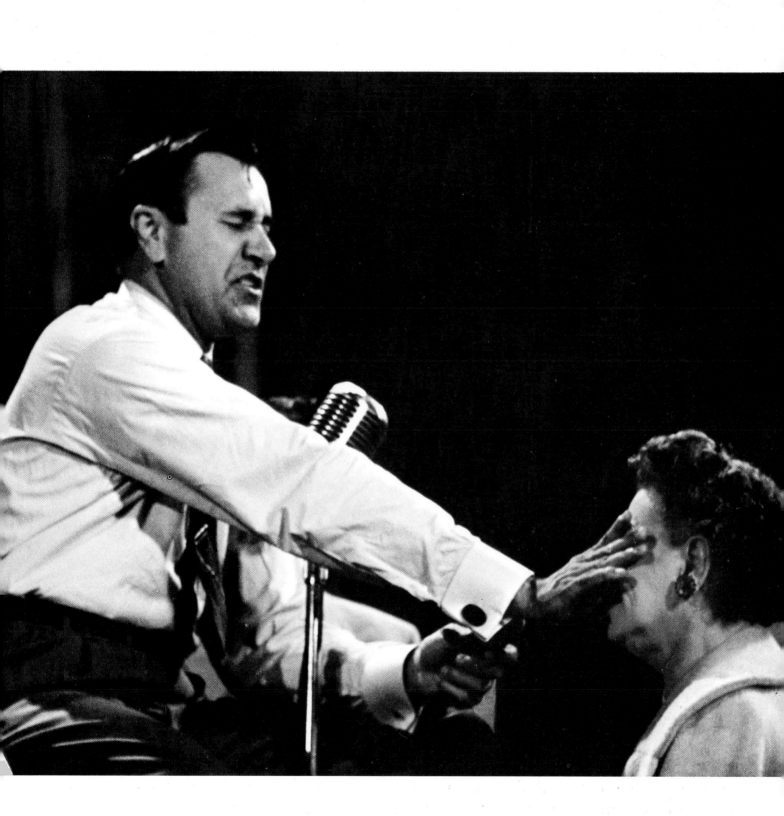

As a photographer, I am always aware of what makes pictures for the documentarian: war, poverty, disaster, ethnic groups, the plight of blacks. They are naturals to the camera. Photographing these things would therefore seem easy for the photographer to choose to do. Actually, because such subjects seem ready-made, the photographer has to strain that much harder to go beyond the obvious. Because I was challenged by these contradictions and because the social aspects of the black problem in America was of prime importance to all of us, black and white, I found myself doing an enormous number of stories on the civil rights movement. It seems to me that if I were asked now what stands out about that time in America, I would say—like a pair of bookends—McCarthyism and the race problem, and between them, the Eisenhower administration's attempt to contain them both by "taking the straight road down the middle."

The civil rights struggle ranged from passive resistance based on Mahatma Gandhi's example in India through Martin Luther King's Alabama bus boycotts to Malcolm X's Black Muslims and their cry for "separation or death."

After the law changed in 1954 from "separate but equal" to integration, the schools became the most dramatic battleground. In 1957, within twenty-four hours of President Eisenhower's sending federal troops, "Little Rock" became part of the international vocabulary.

I always regretted that I chose not to photograph events in Little Rock. At the time, I was concerned with doing features behind the news. I don't like to do hard news. Perhaps it is because I can't stand the ignominy of missing the one possible and often too obvious shot. Or perhaps it is because I can't run fast enough. Behind the scenes, one gets a greater chance for a more perceptive and more intimate look at a situation than one generally does at the event itself.

With this in mind, I went to Virginia where there was a state law that said that if a single black child was admitted to a Virginia public school, the governor had the right to shut down the schoolhouse. It was there that legal action would take place. Lawyers for black students would arrive with petitions to insist upon the constitutional rights of their clients to enroll in desegregated schools.

CORE (Congress of Racial Equality) was representative of group cooperation between blacks and whites. They had set up training facilities throughout the South to teach resistance techniques that would open doors that white bigotry had closed.

I was asked by *Look* to investigate one such training group in Petersburg, Virginia. My editor called the story "School for Sit-ins." Actually, there were sit-ins, pray-ins, wade-ins (at the public white swimming pools). I even heard of a piss-in—so called when two black tenants moved into an all-white building and the landlord cut off their lighting and plumbing. The couple managed with candlelight, a bucket brigade, and a pulley that hoisted up food and lowered refuse.

In Petersburg the Reverend Wyatt T. Walker was preparing picketers for action. The meeting was held in a church. My subject was Priscilla Washington, a black twenty-year-old

biology student from Virginia State College. She was being taught how to picket and to sit-in at a counter at Woolworth's. This was the beginning of economic sanctions. CAN'T EAT–DON'T BUY read her placard.

The group in the church were told, "Passive means non-violent and non-retaliatory. The fact that you can't eat at the same lunch counter as the whites is a reminder that you're inferior. We have to find a device that will change things." The device was to hit the money machine where it hurt, but to do it so that it was effective and did not bring reprisals.

They were also told that night in the church: "Make sure your hair is properly combed and your shoelaces tied, because if you are on that picket line and raise a hand to straighten your hair or bend down to tie your shoes and accidentally jostle a white passer-by, the police will move in."

It was tough training. The next day, still in the church, Priscilla Washington was given a practical lesson in what might happen to her when she sat down at a white lunch counter. Fellow blacks trained for the work acted out the parts of whites. Priscilla was called "biggity nigger" and "black bastard" and remarks like "What you want anyway? Haven't we done enough for you?" were thrown at her while her trainers pulled her hair and a man blew smoke in her face. She stood it stoically for two hours, trying to concentrate on the Bible she was reading.

She passed the test and the next day took up her sign and walked. It was a test of courage, but nothing happened. The police watched her from across the way. I asked her how she managed to

Singing "We Shall Overcome" at Virginia State College with Guy Carawan

keep marching up and down that street for two hours. She said she had recited poetry and chemical formulas.

Her demonstration was an anticlimax. We were told the police decided to keep the vigilantes quiet. We ended the day at Virginia State College. (I no longer remember—was it all black? It would have had to have been the old style "separate but equal.") A white folk singer, Guy Carawan, had come from South Carolina with his guitar. As I looked at these young, determined faces singing "We shall overcome...the truth shall make us free...," I felt sad and ashamed that the coins of equality were literally that—DON'T BUY AT WOOLWORTH'S would get them further than all the inspirational songs going.

In 1959 I had suggested to some editors at *Life* that I do a photo essay on Malcolm X and the Black Muslims. They agreed, and over a period of two years I followed Malcolm X from Washington to New York, to Chicago, and back to New York. It took so long because sessions were random and infrequent. Malcolm was not easy to pin down and I had to be ready to move at his convenience. He made it obvious that he did not like·the white press, but after the first year he must have decided to use them.

In his autobiography he writes that *Life* had tried on numerous occasions to photograph him, but he had refused. In the end, my essay on him did not appear in *Life*—but he did cooperate with me on the story. I quote from a letter I wrote from Chicago to my son, who was at school in England: "I was greeted by Malcolm, Raymond, son-in-law to Elijah Muhammad, head of the Fruit of Islam, and James, head of the mosque in Chicago. We proceeded to go from grocery shop to restaurant, to cleaning establishment, to factory, to bakery—all Muslim-owned and -operated. The big surprise to me in this was Malcolm bringing ten Muslim women in their costumes—veils, long skirts, etc. Malcolm set up the shots and I clicked the camera. It was hilarious. I tried on a couple of occasions to get him in the act of framing a photo with his hands, or just setting one up, but he was too quick for me. A commendable day's work. I shot from 12 noon to 5 steadily."

It was strange to be a white woman at Black Muslim meetings and to hear Elijah Muhammad repeating, "The devil is a white man." It was even stranger to be a Jew at these meetings and to see George Lincoln Rockwell—the head of the American Nazi Party—with his boys in their Nazi uniforms and swastika armbands. I had nightmares about what could happen in the United States if such a party came to power.

Malcolm X

One night in New York, Malcolm invited me to dinner at a restaurant the Black Muslims ran in Harlem. The place was spotless (the Black Muslims were always saying whites didn't bathe and smelled bad). The food was delicious. I was served a pie that in my ignorance I referred to as "sweet potato pie." Malcolm and the waiter froze. When I asked what I had done wrong, Malcolm told me that their religion forbade them to eat "slave food." "Then what," I asked, "is in this pie?" He looked at me. "It's made with white beans." The "white" was underlined in his speech. He said it with such venom that I wondered if it was meant to make me feel like a cannibal.

After dinner I went up to 125th Street to photograph a group that was even more militant than Malcolm's called the African Nationalists. I walked in and out of the posters of a white Jesus and black Jesus. The white one said: "He's the wrong God—he has the wrong hair." The black one said: "He is the right God—he has the right hair." As I walked about, I was spat on and called "white bitch."

It was a mild spring night and I wore a light wool dress and a light wool sweater. Lucky for me my clothes were wool. Wool doesn't burn; it smolders. Later, when I took off my sweater to take the exposed film from its zippered pockets, I saw that the entire back of it was polka-dotted with cigarette burns. As I had moved about the crowd they had stuck burning cigarettes into the

sweater. I must have been moving too fast for them to get to the flesh beneath.

In spite of these adventures, I went on still another trip to Chicago. The purpose was to take pictures of the Black Muslim's independent ventures. In addition to the businesses, they had set up mosques and colleges in which classes were taught in Arabic.

It was midwinter. There was a snowstorm when I got to my deluxe hotel in Chicago. As arranged, I called Malcolm. We agreed that we would start work next morning and that he would call me then to arrange where and when to meet. Next morning at eight o'clock I got a telephone call. A voice with a southern accent said, "Get the hell out of town before it's too late," and hung up. Half an hour later Malcolm called. He was polite but brisk and gave me a time and an address in the black ghetto. I met him four days running. He called me each morning with instructions, but each morning at eight the other voice called and gave me the same message: "Get the hell out of town before it's too late." I don't know why I wasn't frightened, but I wasn't, and although it occurred to me to tell the *Life* bureau in Chicago, I didn't, because I was afraid they would take me off the story and I wanted to follow it to its conclusion.

Among my captions for the pictures, I find the following text: "I talked to an indoctrinated Muslim who had been a cook in a Detroit hotel

Black Muslim graduation

Black Muslim honor guard

before he became a leader in the Fruit of Islam, the elite guard. He said: 'I want my gold shoes now, I want my white robes now, I want my milk and honey right now. I have sung too many songs in the Baptist Church and had too much water poured over me. I want now what the white man has.' Sitting opposite him and looking into those fanatic eyes and seeing the purpose that this movement has given him, I understood. He had looked to me like any other cook, but cleaner; neatly pressed gray flannel suit, neat black tie, polished high yellow shoes. But there is a difference—he has a purpose, a dignity he never had before. And yes, a chance to hold up his head. True, he is given a ready-made heritage and a blinkered channel for his life. He does not question. He does not probe. Allah so wills it. He has an identification with all other black people that are stirring the world over, and Islam which is gaining strength in Africa."

There was an amusing postscript to my troubled Malcolm X story. When it was together and laid out for *Life,* the editors looked at twelve pages of pictures. The editor in charge of it got very nervous and kept saying: "But nobody knows who these people are—why should *Life* magazine do a story on them?" His assistant kept saying: "They look as though they're in Africa. Why should we bother?" I kept interrupting with: "But it's America and it's precisely because nobody knows who they are that we must do them!"

After a great deal of soul searching on the editors' parts and a great deal of fast talking on my part, reminding them of all the time and money they had spent (expenses $10,000), they agreed to send the story to the editorial weekly session where the final decisions are made. The heads of the various departments convene at these and each would try to push his particular subject—foreign news, domestic news, fashion, sports, entertainment, etc. That first editorial conference I lost out—I no longer remember why. The second week it came up for a ten-page layout and went to press. When it came back from the make-ready, they found that the story ended with a horizontal picture half a page deep and running two pages across, and below it, half a page deep and two pages across, was an advertisement. My closing picture was of Elijah Muhammad's wife and daughter at prayer. The advertisement below it was for Oreos, the chocolate cookies. The copy line on the ad read: "The greatest chocolate cookie of them all." *Life* didn't pull the ad; they pulled my story, and we never mentioned it again.

Black Muslim army,
Fruit of Islam

Elijah Muhammad and Malcolm X

Elijah Muhammad's daughter and wife

George Lincoln Rockwell flanked by
members of American Nazi Party at
Black Muslim meeting

As a change from the serious black stories, I did some lighthearted assignments. I went with Bennett Cerf, the Random House publisher and TV personality, to Atlantic City to do a story for *Esquire* on the Miss America contest. The simplest way to go was by train, but Bennett, who liked to present himself in the most dramatic way, decided to fly. Plane transport was considered chic in those days. I had been asked by Arnold Gingrich, the publisher of *Esquire,* to look after Bennett. To me, that was a command, meaning "make him feel important." I went to Atlantic City a day early. I hired a limousine and two off-duty motorcycle cops from the Police Department as outriders (ten bucks each) and when Bennett arrived at the airport—flight time twenty-five minutes—I met him in style and piped him into Atlantic City. He took it as his due. Never questioned it; just assumed the mayor had sent me. I never peeped, and I was too embarrassed to put it on my expense account. It was worth the cost to see such self-assurance.

The Miss America contest didn't quite come under the heading of light entertainment for me. I found it flat and tacky, lacking in style and grace. I found the inspection of the girls' brassieres for "falsies" ludicrous, and I found the new rules requiring the girls to compete in a talent show sad. The girls I saw were neither talented nor sexy. They had a kind of over-all wholesomeness which I found sometimes boring and sometimes fatuous and which somehow belonged to the period.

In the 50's I was too busy recording the events to sort out their meanings. What I thought were unrelated accidents, I see now as roots in the society of the 50's that were to surface later and affect our lives.

For instance, in 1952, when I did a photo essay on a tussle between the Bartenders' Union and the female owner of the 711 Bar in Manhattan over her right to have a woman bartender, I thought it just a funny vignette. Now, when I look at the pictures of the male pickets, I realize that what was at stake was their refusal to have women in their union. Now I can see it against the background of the Women's Movement. If I were doing it now, would I go to the head of the Woman's Christian Temperance Union for her comment and her picture? Probably, because I would still want an interesting picture, even though I know that now, as then, her part in the story was irrelevant.

Owner of 711 Bar

Female bartender

Head of the Woman's Christian Temperance Union

The year was 1960—my last full American photographic year. For *Harper's Bazaar*, I made pictures of the possible presidential candidates' wives—Mrs. Lyndon Johnson, Mrs. Richard Nixon, Mrs. Hubert Humphrey, and Mrs. John F. Kennedy. A lady-editor-with-a-hat-on and I went to Washington, with little suits and black dresses for the ladies to wear for the pictures and which we would pretend they would wear for their mates' election campaigns, if their husbands were nominated.

Two incidents stand out from that day. The first was when we were being escorted back to our car by Mrs. Nixon. I tripped over what I thought was a black rug lying on a sidewalk. It was the dog Checkers. He looked old and ill and moth-eaten. He was then thirteen years old, but considering the famous "Checkers speech" of the 1952 campaign, too important to be put out of his misery.

The other incident had to do with Mrs. Kennedy. I was impressed with her because she refused to wear the dress the editor brought, insisting, and rightly, that her own Givenchy suit was absolutely perfect for her. When we discussed the picture I was to take, I suggested that we take it with Caroline. She was not pleased and kept saying, "Why does everybody want me with the baby?" Actually, the press had not yet gotten to her, and except for the occasional newspaper picture, there hadn't been much about her in the media. I said that I had four pages—one for each of the ladies—and she, the youngest and the prettiest, would be bound to get the lead page, especially if she had the baby. I added, "It will help get votes." She didn't reply, but went to the door to admit Kenneth, her hairdresser. He had flown down from New York to do her hair for the picture. They went upstairs to get her ready and when they came down, she was carrying Caroline. "Where do you want us?" she asked. The light was coming from the back of the house, so I suggested we go there. Mrs. Kennedy opened a door and we were in a charming library. Sitting on a couch were two men. One was interviewing the other, but I was not paying much attention. I was reading the light. Mrs. Kennedy asked me if it was all right. I nodded. She jerked a thumb at the two men, indicating that they were to go upstairs. They rose and started to walk out. The younger of the two opened the door, then turned and walked back, held out his hand to me, and said, "I'd like to introduce myself—my name is John Kennedy."

Mrs. Richard
Nixon

Mrs. Hubert
Humphrey

Mrs. Lyndon
Johnson

Mrs. John F.
Kennedy and
Caroline

I thought of this incident months later when I was working in the Nevada desert on John Huston's film *The Misfits*. Members of the cast and crew had gathered to watch Kennedy and Nixon debate on television. As I remember it, Richard Nixon looked pretty seedy, blue-bearded, and heavy, but John Kennedy looked radiant.

Which of these two was to be the new hero? The old hero's—Eisenhower's—days were over. Long live—?

That night I could not sleep. I kept remembering the 1952 Republican Convention and the practically unknown Nixon, picked by the Eisenhower forces to try to satisfy the right wing of the Republican Party. Now Vice President, Nixon was running his own campaign for President and trying subtly to disengage himself from the disappointing Eisenhower years. He was selling himself to us as an experienced statesman; and the young Kennedy was exploiting his charisma and building his own mythology.

Looking *now* at the *then* I knew, I wonder how (if I had not gone abroad) I would have worked in the United States as a picture journalist in the 60's and 70's. How would I have developed as a photographer? Would I have still tried to record social history as I saw it? Would I have

learned enough about McCarthyism to have been able to report on Vietnam and Watergate, both of which I feel were spawned in the 50's and were not unrelated events?

How would I have recorded other events and situations that had deep roots in the 50's—the destruction of the cities, the unemployment, the violence, the shift of black problems from the South to the cities of the North?

Would I, as so many of my colleagues have done, have found a comfortable way to photograph? The function we once served as investigative reporters with cameras is no longer needed. There are no American magazines to print our pictures. We have lost our showcases. There are no major picture magazines to pay our fees and our expenses. There are mainly magazines that use some pictures. Television has, in a sense, made us redundant, but it has not canceled out still photography.

The paradox is that the still is now an acknowledged art form, hanging in museums and special galleries, viewed by millions of people and collected by those who can pay high prices. It has achieved academic status in the universities. It has become "establishment," with its jargon, its pundits, its critics, its seminars, its beautifully reproduced books, and now its preciousness about limited prints from a single negative. The commercial attempt to make exclusive and elitist that which is endlessly reproducible, I find sad.

I would prefer photography to be a folk art—cheap and available to everybody, rather than elevated to mandarin proportions created through an artificial scarcity. Prices for collectors are in ascending order depending upon whether the print is made from a copy negative or from the original negative; whether the print has been made by a laboratory or by the photographer himself; whether it is unsigned or signed, etc.

It seems that one hundred prints could be cheaply made, at a price that even students could afford, rather than a single, exclusive, exquisite print for one person to file away in a drawer. The going belief is that very few prints are hung—mainly they are put in light-proof drawers to accrue in value.

I want to go back to photographers and to picture journalism. What I knew in America in the 50's was free and adventurous, both in the use of the instrument and in the scope it gave the photographer to range the world in search of subject matter. Although this continued throughout the 60's, very little of that still obtains. There are a few magazines in Europe—in Britain and in a few other countries—that still need the editorial matter to keep the ads apart.

Photographers have gone into industrial work—for annual reports, advertising, film promotion, and various other commercial enterprises—in order to pay the rent. To satisfy their own creative needs, some of them carry an extra camera, loaded with black-and-white film, to shoot what one of them described to me as "my own pictures."

Others do nothing but shoot, in the hope of hanging their work on museum walls or selling it to collectors. In the old days the maxim from the magazine's art department would be something like "Give me one great picture and I'll give you an eight-page layout." Now, when the photographer gets one great picture, he hangs it on a museum wall.

One day while I was still trying to absorb all the changes I saw about me in my field, I called Charles Harbutt, an old friend and a gifted photographer. I was trying to understand the changes and the difference in photography between the 50's and the 70's. "Oh," said Charles, "that's easy—photography in the 50's was about people. Now it's about photography."